MIGHTY MINERALS IN ROCK

by Rex Ruby

Minneapolis, Minnesota

Credits
Cover and title page, © ARCTIC IMAGES /Alamy Stock Photo; 4–5, © Chris LaBasco/iStock; 6, © Dr. Norbert Lange/Shutterstock; 7, © William Mullins/Alamy Stock Photo; 8L, © Givaga/Adobe Stock; 8R, © johannes/Adobe Stock; 9, © Victor/Adobe Stock; 10–11, © Leroy Gibbins Jr/Shutterstock; 12, © RainerPlendl/iStock; 13TL, © Bjoern Wylezich/iStock; 13TR, © kaisphoto/iStock; 13BL, © Roy Palmer/Shutterstock; 13BR, © Alenka00/iStock; 14–15, © ygor/Shutterstock; 16L, © Marco Fine/Shutterstock; 16R, © rep0rter/iStock; 17, © mineral vision/iStock; 18–19, © Moussa81/iStock; 20–21, © gjohnstonphoto/iStock; 22, © ryasick/iStock, © to_csa/iStock, © Lemon_tm/iStock, © vaitekune/iStock, © Anastasiia Burlakova/iStock, © oumjeab/Shutterstock, © nito/Shutterstock, and © BongkarnGraphic/Shutterstock; Used Throughout, © mineral vision/iStock.

Bearport Publishing Company Product Development Team
President: Jen Jenson; Director of Product Development: Spencer Brinker; Managing Editor: Allison Juda; Associate Editor: Naomi Reich; Associate Editor: Tiana Tran; Art Director: Colin O'Dea; Designer: Kim Jones; Designer: Kayla Eggert; Product Development Assistant: Owen Hamlin

Library of Congress Cataloging-in-Publication Data is available at www.loc.gov or upon request from the publisher.

ISBN: 979-8-89232-030-6 (hardcover)
ISBN: 979-8-89232-507-3 (paperback)
ISBN: 979-8-89232-159-4 (ebook)

For more information, write to Bearport Publishing, 5357 Penn Avenue South, Minneapolis, MN 55419.

CONTENTS

LET'S LOOK AT ROCKS

El Capitan towers over everything around it. This huge rock is in Yosemite National Park in California. But other rocks nearby are the size of sand. There are thousands of different kinds of rock on Earth. They come in many different sizes and colors. Some are dull, while others sparkle. These differences all come down to what rocks are made of.

El Capitan is made of a kind of rock called granite (GRAN-it).

El Capitan

MADE OF MINERALS

From a distance, El Capitan looks gray. But if you look more closely, the rock is speckled with black, gray, and white. Under a **microscope**, you would see that the granite is formed of billions of tiny **grains**. Each grain is made of a solid substance called a **mineral**.

Mineral grains can be even smaller than grains of sand.

Mineral grains of granite

The color of granite depends on the types of mineral grains inside it.

WHAT ARE MINERALS?

Minerals form naturally on Earth. When grains of minerals join together, they can make solid rock. Some grains have straight edges, while others have rounded shapes. Straight edges help the grains fit together tightly. Large, round grains are held together by smaller grains. These small grains hold large rocks together like the cement in a brick wall.

Sandstone under a microscope

ROCK INGREDIENTS

There are more than 3,000 different minerals on Earth. Some rocks are made of just one mineral. However, many are a mixture of different minerals. Granite usually contains four or five different minerals. Two common minerals in granite are quartz (KWORTS) and feldspar. Many rocks include quartz as one of their mineral ingredients.

The Rainbow Rock cliffs in Oregon are made of chert (CHURT), which is a kind of rock that contains quartz.

Rainbow Rock cliffs

METALS FROM ROCKS

Some rocks contain pieces of metal. That's because all metals are actually minerals. Most metals are gray and shiny. Many of them, including aluminum (uh-LOO-mi-nuhm), copper, iron, nickel, and silver, are removed from rocks. Then, they are made into objects that people use every day.

Iron is a metal used to make steel. Cars, buses, and trucks are all made from steel.

Bauxite

Aluminum soda cans

Different metals and rocks can be used to make different things.

Galena

Silver jewelry

GLITTERING GOLD

Some rocks contain tiny grains of a metal called gold. Gold is a **rare** mineral that is difficult to find. People first began removing gold from rock thousands of years ago. They used it to make objects, such as coins, statues, and **coffins**. Today, people still use gold to make valuable jewelry.

Gold is the only metal that is naturally yellow.

Tutankhamun, an ancient Egyptian king, was buried in a gold coffin.

COLORFUL CRYSTALS

The minerals in rocks sometimes form **crystals.** Crystals can be tiny and difficult to see in some rocks. In others, they grow larger and form beautiful shapes. Some minerals, such as certain types of quartz, form crystals as clear as glass. Others, such as peridot (PEH-ruh-daht) and sodalite (SOH-duh-lite), create crystals with bright colors.

Amethyst
Straight edge
Smooth face
Crystals have straight edges and smooth sides called faces.

WHAT A GEM!

Mineral crystals are colorful and pretty. These crystals are removed from rocks, cut into shapes, and **polished**. They are used to decorate jewelry and other valuable objects, such as crowns. When we use mineral crystals this way, they are called **gemstones**. Some gemstones found in rocks include diamonds and sapphires (SAF-ires).

Diamonds are hard and tough minerals that are used in tools for cutting glass and metal.

Diamond
Sapphire

MANY ROCKS, MANY MINERALS

From a distance, a rock may look gray and boring—but take a closer look. It might contain colorful crystals, grains of gold, or even a diamond. These differences are what makes learning about rocks and minerals so fun!

People who collect rocks and minerals might search for them on hillsides or beaches. Some buy rocks from shops.

SCIENCE LAB

Mixing Minerals

Using modeling clay, pebbles, and other materials, show how rocks can be made from different mixtures of minerals.

You will need:

- Colorful modeling clay
- Pebbles
- Sand
- Beads
- Buttons
- Glitter

1. Use different colored clay to make small rock-shaped balls.

2. Next, add different mixtures of pebbles, sand, beads, buttons, and glitter to your clay rock balls.

3. Explain to your family and friends how your model rocks are similar to and different from real rocks.

GLOSSARY

coffins containers in which bodies are placed for burial

crystals solid minerals that have formed into shapes with straight edges and smooth sides

gemstones precious minerals, such as diamonds, rubies, or emeralds, that can be found in rocks

grains small, hard pieces of something

microscope a device used to see things that are too small to see with the eyes alone

mineral a solid substance found in nature that makes up rocks

polished made smooth and shiny

rare not often found or seen

INDEX

READ MORE

Daly, Ruth. *How We Use Rocks and Minerals (Introduction to Earth's Resources).* New York: Crabtree Publishing Company, 2021.

McDougal, Anna. *Minerals (Earth's Rocks in Review).* Buffalo, NY: Enslow Publishing, 2024.

LEARN MORE ONLINE

1. Go to **www.factsurfer.com** or scan the QR code below.
2. Enter "**Rockin Minerals**" into the search box.
3. Click on the cover of this book to see a list of websites.

ABOUT THE AUTHOR

Rex Ruby lives in Minnesota with his family. He likes going on long walks and discovering new rocks along the trail.